Table of Contents

Chapter 1: Introduction to AI Innovation in America

The Rise of AI in the US

As the global leader in AI innovation, the United States continues to dominate the AI landscape with significant investments and top-tier AI researchers. In 2023 alone, the US raised an impressive $31 billion across 1,151 deals, solidifying its position as a powerhouse in the AI industry. Major companies like Google, Microsoft, and IBM are at the forefront of AI innovation, driving advancements in various AI applications, including generative AI and industrial automation.

Google, known for its cutting-edge AI research and development, has been making significant strides in the field of AI with projects like DeepMind and TensorFlow. Microsoft, on the other hand, has been focusing on integrating AI into its products and services, such as Azure AI and Microsoft Cognitive Services. IBM, a pioneer in AI research, has been pushing the boundaries of AI technology with projects like Watson and IBM Research AI.

One of the key trends in AI innovation in the US is the rise of generative AI, which has the ability to create new content, images, and even music. Companies like OpenAI and Adobe are leveraging generative AI technology to revolutionize the creative industry, giving rise to new possibilities in content creation and design. Another major trend is industrial automation, where AI is being used to optimize manufacturing processes, improve efficiency, and reduce costs for businesses.

With the US leading the charge in AI innovation, the future looks bright for the AI industry in America. As companies continue to invest in AI research and development, we can expect to see even more groundbreaking advancements in AI technology that will shape the way we live and work in the years to come. The US is well-positioned to remain at the forefront of AI innovation, driving growth and innovation in the AI industry for years to come.

Overview of Major Players in AI

As the United States continues to dominate the AI landscape with significant investments and top-tier AI researchers, major players such as Google, Microsoft, and IBM are leading the charge in AI innovation. These companies have been driving advancements in various AI applications, including generative AI and industrial automation. With a combined total of $31 billion raised across 1,151 deals in 2023, these major players are at the forefront of shaping the future of AI technology.

Google, known for its search engine dominance, has also become a major player in the AI space. With projects like Google Brain, DeepMind, and TensorFlow, Google has been pushing the boundaries of AI research and development. Its advancements in natural language processing, image recognition, and machine learning have revolutionized the way we interact with technology.

Microsoft, another tech giant, has been heavily investing in AI research and development. With projects like Azure AI, Cognitive Services, and Project Bonsai, Microsoft is leveraging AI to drive innovation across various industries. From healthcare to finance to manufacturing, Microsoft's AI solutions are helping businesses optimize processes, improve decision-making, and drive growth.

IBM, a pioneer in the field of AI, has been making significant strides in AI innovation. With projects like Watson, IBM has been at the forefront of developing AI solutions for businesses. Its focus on enterprise AI, cloud-based AI services, and AI-powered automation has positioned IBM as a key player in the AI landscape.

Overall, these major players in AI are not only driving advancements in AI technology but also shaping the future of AI innovation. With their significant investments, top-tier researchers, and groundbreaking projects, Google, Microsoft, and IBM are leading the charge in revolutionizing the way we interact with AI technology.

Trends Shaping the AI Landscape

Artificial Intelligence (AI) is rapidly evolving, and there are several key trends shaping the AI landscape in America. One of the most significant trends is the continued dominance of the US in AI innovation. With significant investments and top-tier AI researchers, the US raised $31 billion across 1,151 deals in 2023. Major companies like Google, Microsoft, and IBM are leading the way in driving advancements in various AI applications, such as generative AI and industrial automation.

Generative AI is a trend that is revolutionizing the way AI systems create content. This technology allows machines to generate realistic images, videos, and text based on a set of input data. Companies are using generative AI to create realistic virtual environments, design products, and even generate human-like speech. This trend has the potential to disrupt various industries, including entertainment, marketing, and design.

Another trend shaping the AI landscape is the increasing focus on industrial automation. Companies are leveraging AI technologies like machine learning and robotics to automate various processes in manufacturing, logistics, and supply chain management. AI-powered robots are being used to perform repetitive tasks more efficiently and accurately, leading to increased productivity and cost savings for businesses. This trend is expected to continue growing as more companies adopt AI-driven automation solutions.

Ethical AI is also a key trend that is gaining momentum in the AI landscape. As AI technologies become more advanced and pervasive, there is a growing concern about the ethical implications of AI systems. Companies are increasingly focusing on developing AI systems that are fair, transparent, and accountable. This trend is driving the adoption of ethical AI principles and frameworks to ensure that AI technologies are used responsibly and ethically.

Overall, the AI landscape in America is dynamic and rapidly evolving, with several key trends shaping the future of AI innovation. From generative AI and industrial automation to ethical AI, companies are leveraging AI technologies to drive advancements and transform industries. As the US continues to dominate the AI landscape, it is essential for companies to stay informed and adapt to these trends to remain competitive in the fast-paced world of AI innovation.

Chapter 2: Google's Impact on AI Innovation

Google's AI Research Labs

Google's AI Research Labs are among the most prominent players in the field of artificial intelligence, with a strong focus on cutting-edge research and development. Google has been at the forefront of AI innovation, driving advancements in various applications such as generative AI and industrial automation. The company's commitment to AI research is evident in the significant investments it has made in this area, which have helped it maintain a competitive edge in the rapidly evolving AI landscape.

One of the key strengths of Google's AI Research Labs is its team of top-tier AI researchers, who are responsible for pushing the boundaries of what is possible in the field of artificial intelligence. These researchers come from diverse backgrounds and bring a wealth of expertise to the table, allowing Google to tackle complex AI challenges with innovative solutions. The company's research labs are equipped with state-of-the-art facilities and resources, enabling researchers to conduct cutting-edge research in areas such as machine learning, natural language processing, and computer vision.

Google's AI Research Labs have also played a crucial role in driving advancements in generative AI, a rapidly growing field that focuses on creating artificial systems capable of generating creative and original content. Google has been at the forefront of research in this area, developing advanced generative models that have the potential to revolutionize industries such as art, music, and design. By harnessing the power of generative AI, Google is paving the way for new forms of creative expression and innovation.

In addition to its work in generative AI, Google's AI Research Labs are also making significant strides in industrial automation, with a focus on developing AI-powered systems that can streamline and optimize manufacturing processes. These systems leverage advanced AI algorithms to improve efficiency, reduce costs, and enhance overall productivity in industries such as automotive, electronics, and aerospace. By harnessing the power of AI, Google is helping to drive the next wave of industrial innovation and transform the way we think about manufacturing.

Overall, Google's AI Research Labs are a driving force behind the company's continued success in the field of artificial intelligence. With a strong focus on research, innovation, and collaboration, Google is well-positioned to remain at the forefront of AI innovation and continue to push the boundaries of what is possible in this rapidly evolving field. As the US continues to dominate the AI landscape, Google's AI Research Labs will undoubtedly play a key role in shaping the future of artificial intelligence and driving advancements in a wide range of industries.

Google's AI Applications

Google is one of the leading players in the field of artificial intelligence, with a wide range of applications across various industries. One of the key areas where Google has made significant strides is in generative AI. Generative AI refers to AI systems that are capable of creating new content, such as images, videos, or text, based on examples provided to them. Google's DeepMind team, for example, has developed a generative AI model called GPT-3, which is known for its ability to produce highly realistic and coherent text.

In addition to generative AI, Google is also heavily involved in the development of AI applications for industrial automation. Industrial automation refers to the use of AI and robotics to streamline and optimize manufacturing processes. Google's parent company, Alphabet, has a division called X, which focuses on moonshot projects, including the development of AI-powered robotics for industrial applications. Google's AI applications in industrial automation have the potential to revolutionize the manufacturing industry by increasing efficiency, reducing costs, and improving overall productivity.

One of the key advantages of Google's AI applications is the company's vast resources and access to a wealth of data. Google is known for its massive data centers and its ability to collect and analyze vast amounts of data, which is crucial for training AI models. This gives Google a significant edge in developing AI applications that are not only accurate but also scalable and reliable. Google's AI applications are also known for their user-friendly interfaces, making them accessible to a wide range of users, from tech-savvy developers to non-technical professionals.

Google's AI applications have the potential to transform a wide range of industries, from healthcare to finance to transportation. In healthcare, for example, Google's AI algorithms are being used to analyze medical images, diagnose diseases, and develop personalized treatment plans. In finance, Google's AI applications are being used to detect fraud, predict market trends, and automate trading strategies. In transportation, Google's AI algorithms are being used to optimize traffic flow, reduce congestion, and improve safety on the roads.

Overall, Google's AI applications are at the forefront of innovation in the field of artificial intelligence. With its vast resources, top-tier researchers, and commitment to pushing the boundaries of AI technology, Google is well-positioned to continue driving advancements in generative AI, industrial automation, and other key AI applications. The US continues to dominate the AI landscape, and companies like Google are leading the way in shaping the future of AI innovation.

Google's Contributions to Generative AI

Google has been a major player in the field of generative AI, making significant contributions to advancements in this area. Generative AI refers to a type of artificial intelligence that has the capability to create new content, such as images, videos, or text, that is similar to the original data it was trained on. Google has been at the forefront of developing generative AI models that have been used in various applications, such as image synthesis, text generation, and even art creation.

One of Google's most notable contributions to generative AI is the development of the GAN (Generative Adversarial Network) model. GANs are a type of generative AI model that consists of two neural networks - a generator and a discriminator - that work together to generate new data that is indistinguishable from the original data. Google has been instrumental in advancing the capabilities of GANs, leading to breakthroughs in image generation, text-to-image synthesis, and even deepfake technology.

Google has also made significant strides in the field of natural language processing (NLP) with its development of advanced language models such as BERT (Bidirectional Encoder Representations from Transformers) and GPT (Generative Pre-trained Transformer). These language models have revolutionized the way AI systems understand and generate human language, enabling applications such as language translation, text summarization, and conversational AI.

In addition to its research and development efforts, Google has also made its generative AI technologies accessible to the broader AI community through open-sourcing its models and tools. This has allowed researchers and developers around the world to leverage Google's advancements in generative AI to drive innovation in various industries, from healthcare to entertainment.

Overall, Google's contributions to generative AI have been instrumental in pushing the boundaries of what is possible with artificial intelligence. With its cutting-edge research, groundbreaking models, and commitment to open collaboration, Google continues to be a driving force in shaping the future of AI innovation in America and beyond.

Chapter 3: Microsoft's Role in AI Advancements

Microsoft's AI Ventures

Microsoft's AI Ventures is a strategic initiative by the tech giant to invest in promising artificial intelligence startups and accelerate innovation in the AI space. With a focus on nurturing and supporting early-stage companies working on cutting-edge AI technologies, Microsoft's AI Ventures program plays a crucial role in shaping the future of AI innovation in America.

Through AI Ventures, Microsoft provides startups with access to its vast resources, including cloud computing infrastructure, data analytics tools, and AI research expertise. By partnering with Microsoft, these startups gain valuable mentorship, guidance, and networking opportunities that help them scale and grow their businesses in the competitive AI market.

One of the key objectives of Microsoft's AI Ventures program is to identify and invest in startups that are developing disruptive AI solutions with the potential to transform industries and drive economic growth. By supporting these high-potential companies, Microsoft is not only fostering innovation but also creating new opportunities for job creation and economic development in the AI sector.

Microsoft's AI Ventures has already made significant investments in a diverse range of AI startups, spanning industries such as healthcare, finance, manufacturing, and cybersecurity. These investments have helped fuel the development of groundbreaking AI technologies that are revolutionizing how businesses operate and deliver value to their customers.

Overall, Microsoft's AI Ventures program is a testament to the company's commitment to driving AI innovation in America and leading the charge in shaping the future of AI technology. By investing in and supporting the next generation of AI startups, Microsoft is playing a pivotal role in accelerating the growth and adoption of AI technologies across industries, ultimately shaping the AI landscape for years to come.

Microsoft's AI Products and Services

Microsoft is one of the major players in the AI landscape, consistently pushing the boundaries of innovation with its AI products and services. From intelligent virtual assistants like Cortana to machine learning platforms like Azure ML, Microsoft offers a wide range of AI solutions for businesses and consumers alike. These products and services are designed to help organizations harness the power of AI to drive efficiencies, improve decision-making, and enhance customer experiences.

One of Microsoft's flagship AI products is Azure Cognitive Services, a suite of APIs and services that enable developers to easily integrate AI capabilities into their applications. With services like computer vision, speech recognition, and natural language processing, Azure Cognitive Services empowers developers to build intelligent applications that can see, hear, speak, and understand natural language. This suite of AI tools has been instrumental in accelerating the adoption of AI across various industries, from healthcare to finance to retail.

In addition to its AI platforms, Microsoft also offers AI-powered products like Dynamics 365 AI, which leverages AI to drive business insights and enhance customer engagement. With features like predictive lead scoring, sentiment analysis, and virtual agents, Dynamics 365 AI enables businesses to unlock valuable insights from their data and deliver personalized experiences to their customers. This product has been instrumental in helping organizations drive growth, improve customer satisfaction, and stay ahead of the competition in today's digital age.

Microsoft's commitment to AI innovation is further evidenced by its investments in research and development. The company has established AI research labs around the world, staffed with top-tier AI researchers and experts who are working on cutting-edge AI technologies. These researchers collaborate with academia, industry partners, and startups to advance the field of AI and bring new innovations to market. Microsoft's AI research efforts have led to breakthroughs in areas like deep learning, reinforcement learning, and natural language processing, shaping the future of AI and driving new possibilities for businesses and society.

Overall, Microsoft's AI products and services are playing a crucial role in driving AI innovation in America and beyond. With its comprehensive suite of AI tools, platforms, and services, Microsoft is empowering businesses to harness the power of AI and unlock new opportunities for growth and success. As the US continues to dominate the AI landscape, Microsoft's contributions to AI innovation are helping to shape the future of AI and drive advancements in various AI applications, from generative AI to industrial automation.

Microsoft's Influence on Industrial Automation

In recent years, Microsoft has played a significant role in shaping the landscape of industrial automation through the use of artificial intelligence. With its advanced technologies and innovative solutions, Microsoft has been able to revolutionize the way industries operate, increasing efficiency and productivity. By leveraging AI capabilities, Microsoft has enabled businesses to automate repetitive tasks, analyze data in real-time, and make informed decisions quickly.

One of the key contributions of Microsoft to industrial automation is its Azure AI platform, which provides a wide range of AI services that can be easily integrated into existing systems. This platform allows companies to develop custom AI solutions tailored to their specific needs, whether it's predictive maintenance, quality control, or supply chain optimization. By empowering businesses with the tools to harness the power of AI, Microsoft has helped drive significant advancements in industrial automation.

Moreover, Microsoft's influence on industrial automation extends beyond its AI platform, as the company continues to invest in research and development to push the boundaries of what is possible. Through partnerships with leading industrial companies, Microsoft has been able to implement AI-driven solutions that have transformed traditional manufacturing processes. From smart factories to autonomous vehicles, Microsoft's technologies are reshaping the future of industrial automation.

Furthermore, Microsoft's commitment to ethical AI practices has also been instrumental in shaping the industry's approach to automation. By prioritizing transparency, accountability, and fairness in AI algorithms, Microsoft is setting a high standard for responsible AI deployment in industrial settings. This focus on ethical considerations ensures that AI technologies are used in a way that benefits society as a whole, while minimizing potential risks and biases.

Overall, Microsoft's influence on industrial automation is undeniable, as the company continues to drive innovation and transformation in the industry. With its cutting-edge AI technologies, commitment to ethical practices, and strategic partnerships, Microsoft is paving the way for a future where intelligent automation is the norm. As industries continue to adopt AI solutions, Microsoft will undoubtedly remain a key player in shaping the future of industrial automation.

Chapter 4: IBM's Leadership in AI Development

IBM's Watson AI Platform

IBM's Watson AI Platform is one of the leading artificial intelligence systems in the world, known for its ability to analyze massive amounts of data and provide insights that can help businesses make more informed decisions. Developed by IBM, Watson uses advanced machine learning and natural language processing algorithms to understand and interpret complex information in a way that is similar to how humans think.

One of the key features of the Watson AI Platform is its cognitive computing capabilities, which allow it to learn from experience and improve its performance over time. This has made Watson particularly well-suited for applications in industries such as healthcare, finance, and customer service, where the ability to process and analyze vast amounts of data quickly and accurately is crucial.

In recent years, IBM has continued to invest heavily in the development of the Watson AI Platform, expanding its capabilities and integrating it with other IBM technologies to create a more comprehensive AI ecosystem. This has led to the creation of new tools and services that leverage Watson's advanced capabilities, such as virtual agents, chatbots, and predictive analytics.

One of the key advantages of the Watson AI Platform is its scalability, allowing businesses of all sizes to access and leverage its powerful capabilities. This has helped democratize AI technology and made it more accessible to organizations that may not have the resources to develop their own AI systems from scratch.

Overall, IBM's Watson AI Platform has been instrumental in driving advancements in AI innovation and shaping the future of artificial intelligence in America. With its advanced capabilities and ongoing investment in research and development, IBM is poised to remain a key player in the AI landscape for years to come.

IBM's AI Solutions for Businesses

IBM is one of the major players in the AI landscape, leveraging its expertise and resources to develop cutting-edge AI solutions for businesses. With a focus on driving advancements in various AI applications, IBM has been at the forefront of innovation in the industry. From generative AI to industrial automation, IBM's AI solutions are designed to help businesses improve efficiency, reduce costs, and drive growth.

One of IBM's key AI solutions for businesses is Watson, a cognitive computing system that can process large amounts of data and provide insights that can help businesses make informed decisions. Watson is used in various industries, including healthcare, finance, and retail, to analyze data, identify patterns, and make predictions. By leveraging Watson, businesses can gain a competitive edge and drive innovation in their respective industries.

Another AI solution offered by IBM is IBM Cloud Pak for Data, a data and AI platform that enables businesses to collect, organize, and analyze data from various sources. With IBM Cloud Pak for Data, businesses can harness the power of AI to gain valuable insights, optimize processes, and make data-driven decisions. This platform is designed to help businesses unlock the full potential of their data and drive digital transformation.

IBM also offers AI-powered automation solutions that can help businesses streamline processes, improve productivity, and reduce costs. From robotic process automation (RPA) to AI-powered chatbots, IBM's automation solutions are designed to help businesses automate repetitive tasks, enhance customer service, and drive efficiency. By implementing these AI-powered automation solutions, businesses can free up resources, increase operational efficiency, and focus on strategic initiatives.

Overall, IBM's AI solutions for businesses are designed to help organizations harness the power of AI and drive innovation in their respective industries. With a focus on generative AI, industrial automation, and other AI applications, IBM is at the forefront of AI innovation, helping businesses unlock new opportunities and drive growth in the digital age.

IBM's Contributions to AI Ethics and Regulations

In recent years, IBM has emerged as a key player in the development of AI ethics and regulations. As a company with a long history of technological innovation, IBM has recognized the importance of ensuring that AI systems are developed and deployed in an ethical manner. In response to growing concerns about the impact of AI on society, IBM has taken proactive steps to address these issues and contribute to the development of ethical guidelines for the use of AI technology.

One of IBM's most notable contributions to AI ethics is the development of the AI Ethics Board. This board is comprised of experts from a variety of fields, including ethics, law, and technology, who work together to develop guidelines and best practices for the responsible use of AI. By bringing together diverse perspectives, IBM is able to ensure that its AI systems are developed in a way that is ethical and in line with societal values.

In addition to its work on the AI Ethics Board, IBM has also been actively involved in shaping public policy around AI regulation. The company has worked closely with policymakers at the local, state, and federal levels to advocate for regulations that promote the responsible use of AI technology. By engaging with policymakers, IBM is able to ensure that its AI systems are developed and deployed in a way that is consistent with legal and ethical standards.

IBM's commitment to AI ethics and regulations is further demonstrated by its investment in research and development in this area. The company has dedicated significant resources to studying the ethical implications of AI technology and developing tools and frameworks to ensure that its AI systems are used in a responsible manner. By investing in research and development, IBM is able to stay ahead of emerging ethical challenges and ensure that its AI technology is developed in a way that benefits society as a whole.

Overall, IBM's contributions to AI ethics and regulations are a testament to the company's commitment to developing AI technology in a responsible and ethical manner. By working with experts, policymakers, and the public, IBM is able to ensure that its AI systems are developed in a way that promotes the well-being of society and upholds the values of transparency, fairness, and accountability. As AI technology continues to advance, IBM's leadership in this area will be crucial in shaping the future of AI innovation in America.

Chapter 5: Emerging Trends in AI Innovation

The Future of Generative AI

Generative AI, a subset of artificial intelligence that focuses on creating new content rather than just analyzing existing data, is poised to revolutionize various industries in the coming years. With major companies like Google, Microsoft, and IBM leading the way in AI innovation, the future of generative AI looks promising. These companies are investing heavily in research and development to push the boundaries of what is possible with generative AI, paving the way for groundbreaking advancements in fields such as healthcare, entertainment, and marketing.

One area where generative AI is expected to have a significant impact is in the field of healthcare. By leveraging generative AI algorithms, researchers and medical professionals can generate synthetic data to simulate different medical scenarios, enabling more accurate diagnoses and treatment plans. This has the potential to revolutionize the way diseases are diagnosed and treated, leading to better patient outcomes and reduced healthcare costs.

In the entertainment industry, generative AI is already being used to create realistic virtual characters and environments for movies, video games, and virtual reality experiences. With further advancements in generative AI technology, we can expect to see even more immersive and engaging entertainment experiences in the future. This could include personalized content tailored to individual preferences, creating a more interactive and personalized entertainment landscape.

In the marketing industry, generative AI is being used to create personalized content and advertisements tailored to individual consumers. By analyzing vast amounts of data, generative AI algorithms can generate highly targeted marketing campaigns that resonate with specific audiences, leading to higher conversion rates and increased sales. As generative AI technology continues to advance, we can expect to see even more personalized and engaging marketing strategies in the future.

Overall, the future of generative AI is bright, with endless possibilities for innovation and advancement. As major players in the AI industry continue to invest in research and development, we can expect to see even more groundbreaking applications of generative AI in the years to come. From healthcare to entertainment to marketing, generative AI has the potential to revolutionize industries and improve the way we live and work.

Impact of AI on Industrial Automation

The impact of AI on industrial automation cannot be overstated, as it has revolutionized the way manufacturers operate and produce goods. With major companies like Google, Microsoft, and IBM leading the charge in AI innovation, advancements in industrial automation have become more sophisticated and efficient than ever before. These companies are investing heavily in research and development to create AI-powered systems that can optimize production processes, reduce downtime, and improve overall productivity in manufacturing facilities.

One of the key benefits of AI in industrial automation is the ability to predict and prevent equipment failures before they occur. By utilizing machine learning algorithms, manufacturers can analyze vast amounts of data from sensors and other sources to identify patterns that indicate potential issues with machinery. This proactive approach to maintenance not only saves time and money but also helps prevent costly downtime that can impact production schedules.

Another significant impact of AI on industrial automation is the increased level of customization and personalization that can be achieved in manufacturing processes. AI algorithms can analyze customer data and preferences to tailor products to individual needs, leading to higher customer satisfaction and loyalty. This level of customization would be impossible without the power of AI to process and analyze vast amounts of data in real-time.

Furthermore, AI in industrial automation enables manufacturers to streamline their operations and improve overall efficiency. By automating repetitive tasks and optimizing workflows, AI-powered systems can help reduce waste, minimize errors, and increase output. This not only benefits the bottom line but also allows manufacturers to focus on more strategic initiatives that drive growth and innovation.

Overall, the impact of AI on industrial automation is undeniable, with major companies in the US leading the way in developing cutting-edge solutions that transform the manufacturing industry. As AI continues to evolve and improve, we can expect to see even greater advancements in industrial automation that will drive productivity, efficiency, and innovation in the years to come.

Ethical Considerations in AI Development

Ethical considerations in AI development are critical as technology continues to evolve and play a significant role in our daily lives. With the US dominating the AI landscape and leading in investments and research, it is essential to address the ethical implications of AI innovation. As major companies like Google, Microsoft, and IBM drive advancements in various AI applications, including generative AI and industrial automation, it is crucial to prioritize ethical considerations in the development process.

One of the key ethical considerations in AI development is the potential for bias in algorithms. AI systems are only as good as the data they are trained on, and if that data is biased, it can lead to discriminatory outcomes. It is essential for developers to be aware of bias in AI algorithms and take steps to mitigate it to ensure fair and unbiased results. This can involve diverse and inclusive data sets, as well as ongoing monitoring and evaluation of AI systems for bias.

Another ethical consideration in AI development is transparency and accountability. As AI systems become more complex and autonomous, it can be challenging to understand how they arrive at decisions. Developers must prioritize transparency in AI algorithms, making it clear how decisions are made and ensuring accountability for those decisions. This can help build trust with users and ensure that AI systems are used responsibly.

Privacy is also a significant ethical consideration in AI development. As AI systems collect and analyze vast amounts of data, there is a risk of infringing on individuals' privacy rights. Developers must prioritize data protection and privacy in AI systems, implementing strong security measures and adhering to data protection regulations. This can help ensure that user data is handled responsibly and ethically in AI development.

Overall, ethical considerations in AI development are essential to ensure that technology is used responsibly and benefits society as a whole. With the US leading in AI innovation, it is crucial for companies and researchers to prioritize ethics in the development process. By addressing bias, promoting transparency and accountability, and protecting user privacy, we can ensure that AI systems are developed and used in a way that aligns with ethical principles and values.

Chapter 6: Conclusion and Future Outlook

Key Takeaways from Top Players in AI

In the fast-paced world of artificial intelligence, it is crucial to stay informed about the latest trends and advancements. The United States continues to lead the way in AI innovation, with major companies like Google, Microsoft, and IBM making significant investments in research and development. These companies are at the forefront of driving advancements in various AI applications, including generative AI and industrial automation.

One key takeaway from top players in AI is the importance of investing in research and development. Google, Microsoft, and IBM have dedicated teams of top-tier AI researchers who are constantly pushing the boundaries of what is possible with AI technology. By investing in R&D, these companies are able to stay ahead of the competition and continue to drive innovation in the field.

Another key takeaway is the focus on collaboration and partnerships. In order to succeed in the highly competitive AI landscape, companies must be willing to work together to share knowledge and resources. Google, Microsoft, and IBM have all formed partnerships with other leading companies in the industry to collaborate on cutting-edge AI projects.

Additionally, top players in AI understand the importance of diversity and inclusion in the field. By bringing together individuals from diverse backgrounds and perspectives, companies are able to foster creativity and innovation. Google, Microsoft, and IBM have all made efforts to promote diversity and inclusion within their organizations, leading to more innovative solutions and a better work environment for all employees.

Overall, the key takeaways from top players in AI highlight the importance of investing in research and development, fostering collaboration and partnerships, and promoting diversity and inclusion. By following these principles, companies can continue to drive advancements in AI technology and stay at the forefront of innovation in the field.

Predictions for the Future of AI Innovation in America

As we look towards the future of AI innovation in America, it is clear that the landscape is rapidly evolving. With the US continuing to dominate the AI market, it is expected that investments in this sector will only continue to grow. In 2023 alone, the US raised an impressive $31 billion across 1,151 deals, highlighting the significant interest and investment in AI technologies.

Major companies such as Google, Microsoft, and IBM are leading the charge in AI innovation, driving advancements in various applications such as generative AI and industrial automation. These companies have the resources and expertise to push the boundaries of what is possible with AI, paving the way for new innovations and breakthroughs in the field.

One of the key predictions for the future of AI in America is the increased integration of AI technologies across industries. As businesses continue to recognize the value of AI in improving efficiency and driving growth, we can expect to see a surge in AI adoption across various sectors. From healthcare to finance to manufacturing, AI will play a crucial role in transforming how businesses operate and deliver value to their customers.

Another prediction for the future of AI in America is the rise of AI-powered personalized experiences. With advancements in machine learning and deep learning algorithms, AI is increasingly being used to personalize services and products for individual users. This trend is expected to continue as companies strive to deliver more tailored and relevant experiences to their customers.

Overall, the future of AI innovation in America looks promising, with continued investment, research, and advancements driving the growth of this dynamic field. As major players like Google, Microsoft, and IBM continue to push the boundaries of what is possible with AI, we can expect to see new applications, technologies, and opportunities emerge that will shape the future of AI in America and beyond.

Recommendations for Businesses and Researchers in the AI Space

As businesses and researchers in the AI space, it is crucial to stay ahead of the curve and capitalize on the opportunities presented by the rapidly evolving landscape of artificial intelligence. With the US dominating the AI market and major companies like Google, Microsoft, and IBM leading the way in innovation, it is essential to keep up with the latest trends and technologies to remain competitive.

One of the key recommendations for businesses in the AI space is to invest in top-tier AI researchers and talent. Hiring skilled professionals with expertise in artificial intelligence can give companies a competitive edge and help drive innovation in AI applications. Additionally, fostering a culture of collaboration and continuous learning within the organization can lead to breakthroughs in AI technology and solutions.

Another important recommendation for businesses in the AI space is to focus on developing AI applications that address real-world challenges and have a positive impact on society. By aligning AI initiatives with social and environmental goals, companies can not only drive innovation but also contribute to the greater good. This approach can also enhance brand reputation and attract top talent who are passionate about making a difference through AI.

For researchers in the AI space, it is crucial to collaborate with industry partners and leverage their expertise and resources to accelerate the development and deployment of AI solutions. By working closely with businesses, researchers can ensure that their work is not only cutting-edge but also relevant and impactful in the real world. This collaboration can also lead to new opportunities for funding, research grants, and commercialization of AI technologies.

In conclusion, the AI landscape in America is thriving, with significant investments and top-tier researchers driving innovation in various applications. To succeed in this competitive environment, businesses and researchers must prioritize talent acquisition, collaboration, and a focus on real-world impact. By following these recommendations, companies and researchers can stay at the forefront of AI innovation and contribute to the continued growth and success of the AI industry in the US.

As of 2024, several countries are leading the way in AI research, investment, and technological advancements:

1. **United States**: The US continues to dominate the AI landscape with significant investments and top-tier AI researchers. It raised $31 billion across 1,151 deals in 2023. Major companies like Google, Microsoft, and IBM are at the forefront of AI innovation, driving advancements in various AI applications, including generative AI and industrial automation.
2. **China**: China is another key player in AI, with substantial government and private investments. Companies like Tencent, Huawei, and Baidu are leaders in AI innovation, developing large language models and other AI technologies. The Chinese government is heavily investing in AI, with expectations of reaching $38.1 billion by 2027.
3. **United Kingdom**: The UK is the third-largest AI market globally, with a valuation expected to reach $1 trillion by 2035. It hosts leading AI development labs like DeepMind and has a strong focus on AI research and development, supported by substantial government investments.
4. **Israel**: Known for its vibrant tech scene, Israel has a significant number of AI startups and strong private investment in AI. The country focuses on developing AI-driven cybersecurity and enterprise solutions.
5. **Canada**: Canada has emerged as a top player in AI research, with significant investments and government support. Key companies include Cohere and Coveo, contributing to Canada's growing influence in the AI sector.
6. **France**: France is a leading contributor to AI research in the European Union, with a diverse range of AI startups and substantial private investments. The government is also committed to fostering AI development through significant funding.
7. **India**: India is a major contributor to AI research in South Asia, with a high penetration rate of AI skills and substantial investments in AI startups. The government is actively promoting AI through initiatives like the upcoming India AI program.
8. **Japan**: Japan plays a critical role in AI development, particularly in robotics and generative AI. It has a strong ecosystem of AI startups and significant investments in AI technologies.
9. **Germany**: Germany is a significant player in AI with a robust startup ecosystem and considerable private investments. The government is also increasing its funding for AI research and development.
10. **Singapore**: Singapore is a leading AI hub in Southeast Asia, with a strong focus on AI research and a supportive government policy framework.

Here's a detailed overview of the AI landscape in each leading country that a leader of an organization would need to know:

United States

AI Strengths:

- **Investment**: The US is the global leader in AI investment, with $31 billion raised in 2023 (Techopedia).
- **Companies**: Major companies like Google, Microsoft, IBM, and numerous startups drive AI innovation. They are involved in various AI applications, including machine learning, generative AI, and industrial automation (Techopedia).
- **Research**: The US has a significant number of top-tier AI researchers and institutions like MIT, Stanford, and Carnegie Mellon, contributing to cutting-edge AI research and development (AI Index).

Government Support:

- The US government actively supports AI development with significant investments, such as $3.3 billion in 2022 (Techopedia).
- Recent regulatory actions include President Biden's Executive Order on AI, highlighting the growing focus on ethical AI practices (AI Index).

China

AI Strengths:

- **Investment**: China is a major player with $95 billion in private AI investments between 2022 and 2023 (Techopedia).
- **Companies**: Leading firms like Tencent, Huawei, and Baidu are at the forefront, developing advanced AI technologies such as large language models (LLMs) (Techopedia).
- **Government Support**: The Chinese government is heavily investing in AI, with plans to reach $38.1 billion by 2027, aiming to become a global AI leader (Techopedia).

Strategic Focus:

- Emphasis on AI for national security, economic growth, and technological independence (Hostinger).

United Kingdom

AI Strengths:

- **Market Size**: The UK is the third-largest AI market globally, valued at $21 billion and projected to reach $1 trillion by 2035 (Techopedia).
- **Companies**: Prominent AI firms include DeepMind and Darktrace, which focus on AI research and cybersecurity (Techopedia).
- **Research**: The UK boasts strong academic institutions and research labs contributing to AI advancements (AI Index).

Government Support:

- The UK government is increasing investment in AI research and infrastructure, including a £100 million supercomputer facility in partnership with Hewlett Packard Enterprise and Bristol University (Techopedia).

Israel

AI Strengths:

- **Innovation Hub**: Israel has a robust tech ecosystem with 144 AI-related startups and $11 billion in private investment between 2013-2022 (Techopedia).
- **Companies**: Notable firms include AI21 Labs, Deep Instinct, and SentinelOne, focusing on AI-driven cybersecurity and enterprise solutions (Techopedia).

Government Support:

- The Israeli government is investing in AI applications, particularly in Hebrew and Arabic, to foster local innovation (Techopedia).

Canada

AI Strengths:

- **Investment**: Canada saw $8.64 billion in AI investment between 2022 and 2023 (Techopedia).
- **Companies**: Leading AI firms include Cohere, Scale AI, and Coveo, which focus on enterprise AI solutions and generative AI platforms (Techopedia).

Government Support:

- The Canadian government is committed to responsible AI development, with over $124 million invested in AI research at the Université de Montréal in 2023 (Techopedia).

France

AI Strengths:

- **Investment**: France raised $1.5 billion in 2023 across 70 deals, with significant contributions from startups like Mistral AI and Braincube (Techopedia).
- **Companies**: Leading firms include Hugging Face and Armis, specializing in open-source AI and cybersecurity (Techopedia).

Government Support:

- President Emmanuel Macron has committed €500 million to foster AI development and create new AI "champions" (Techopedia).

India

AI Strengths:

- **Investment**: India raised $3.24 billion in AI investments last year, highlighting its growing influence in the AI sector (Techopedia).
- **Companies**: Key players include Avaamo, HEAPS, and SigTuple, focusing on conversational AI, healthcare AI, and automation (Techopedia).

Government Support:

- The Indian government plans to launch the India AI program to boost local AI startups and innovation (Techopedia).

Japan

AI Strengths:

- **Investment**: Japan has invested $4 billion in AI between 2013-2022, with significant funding in 2023 (Techopedia).

- **Companies**: Leading firms include SoftBank Robotics and Preferred Networks, specializing in robotics and autonomous vehicles (Techopedia).

Government Support:

- Japan plans to invest 2 trillion yen ($13 billion) into semiconductor and AI development (Techopedia).

Germany

AI Strengths:

- **Investment**: Germany raised $1.4 billion in AI funding in 2023 across 71 deals (Techopedia).
- **Companies**: Notable AI firms include Aleph Alpha, Orbem, and DeepL, focusing on LLMs, AI translation, and autonomous mobility (Techopedia).

Government Support:

- The German government is doubling its AI research funding, pledging nearly €1 billion towards AI solutions (Techopedia).

Singapore

AI Strengths:

- **Investment**: Singapore has generated $5 billion in AI investment between 2013-2022 (Techopedia).
- **Companies**: The region hosts 165 AI startups, focusing on diverse applications from healthcare to finance (Techopedia).

Government Support:

- The Singapore government is committed to AI development, with significant funding and supportive policies (Hostinger).

www.ingramcontent.com/pod-product-compliance
Lightning Source LLC
Chambersburg PA
CBHW080424240526
45472CB00022B/2307

ISBN 9798328530262

SERENITY STROKES: DELICATE DESIGNS FOR RELAXATION